Who's Watching Over Me?

TRILOGY
A WHOLLY OWNED SUBSIDIARY OF TBN
PROFESSIONAL PUBLISHING MEETS POWERFUL PROMOTION

Trilogy Christian Publishers
A Wholly Owned Subsidiary of Trinity Broadcasting Network
2442 Michelle Drive
Tustin, CA 92780

Copyright © 2024 by Teresa Savage

All rights reserved, including the right to reproduce this book or portions thereof in any form whatsoever.

For information, address Trilogy Christian Publishing
Rights Department, 2442 Michelle Drive, Tustin, CA 92780.
Trilogy Christian Publishing/ TBN and colophon are trademarks of Trinity Broadcasting Network.

For information about special discounts for bulk purchases, please contact Trilogy Christian Publishing.

Trilogy Disclaimer: The views and content expressed in this book are those of the author and may not necessarily reflect the views and doctrine of Trilogy Christian Publishing or the Trinity Broadcasting Network.

10 9 8 7 6 5 4 3 2 1

Library of Congress Cataloging-in-Publication Data is available.

ISBN 979-8-89041-365-9
ISBN 979-8-89041-366-6 (ebook)

Who's Watching Over Me?

Teresa Savage

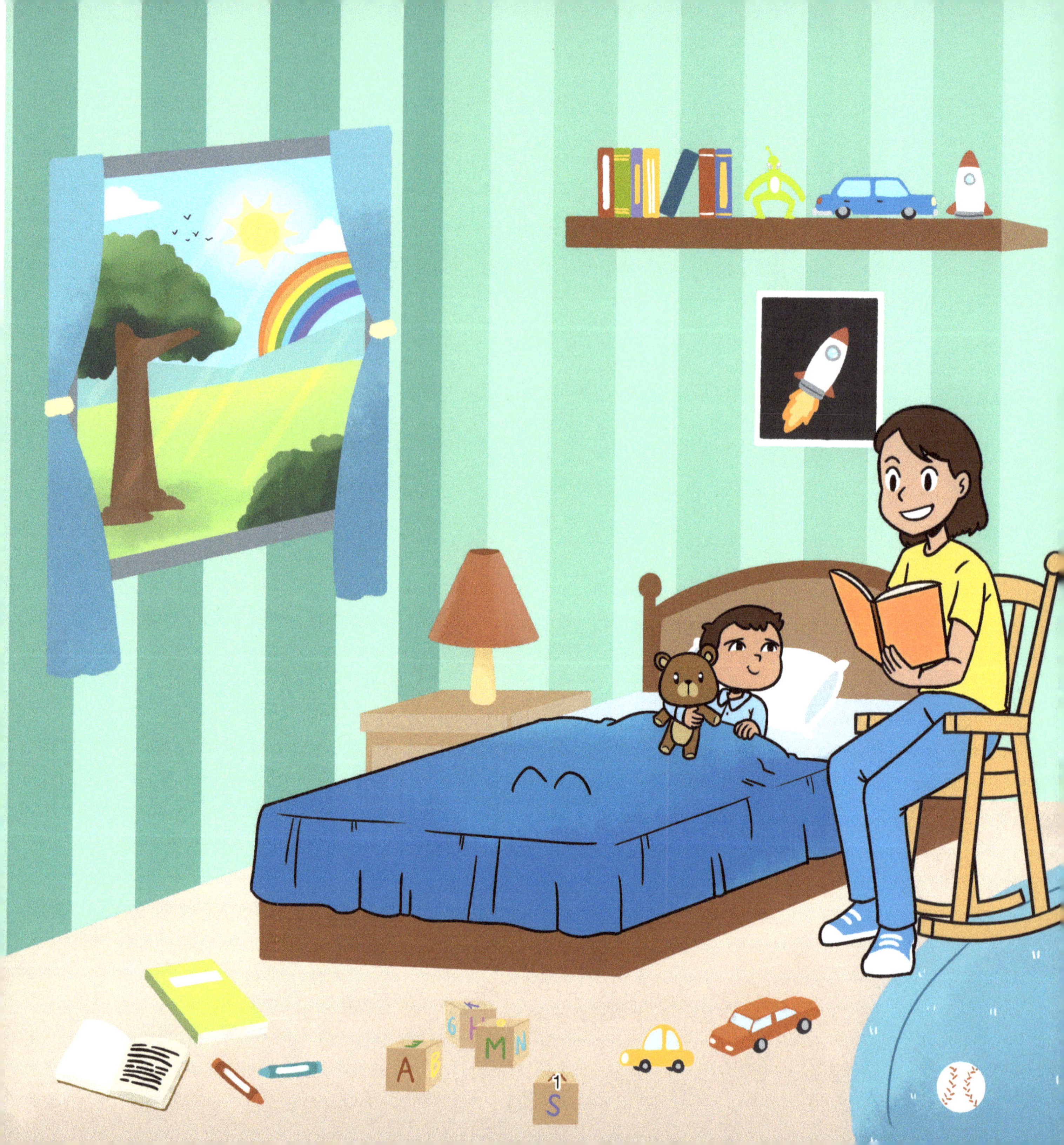

Time to sleep, little one. Remember, we are all watching over you.

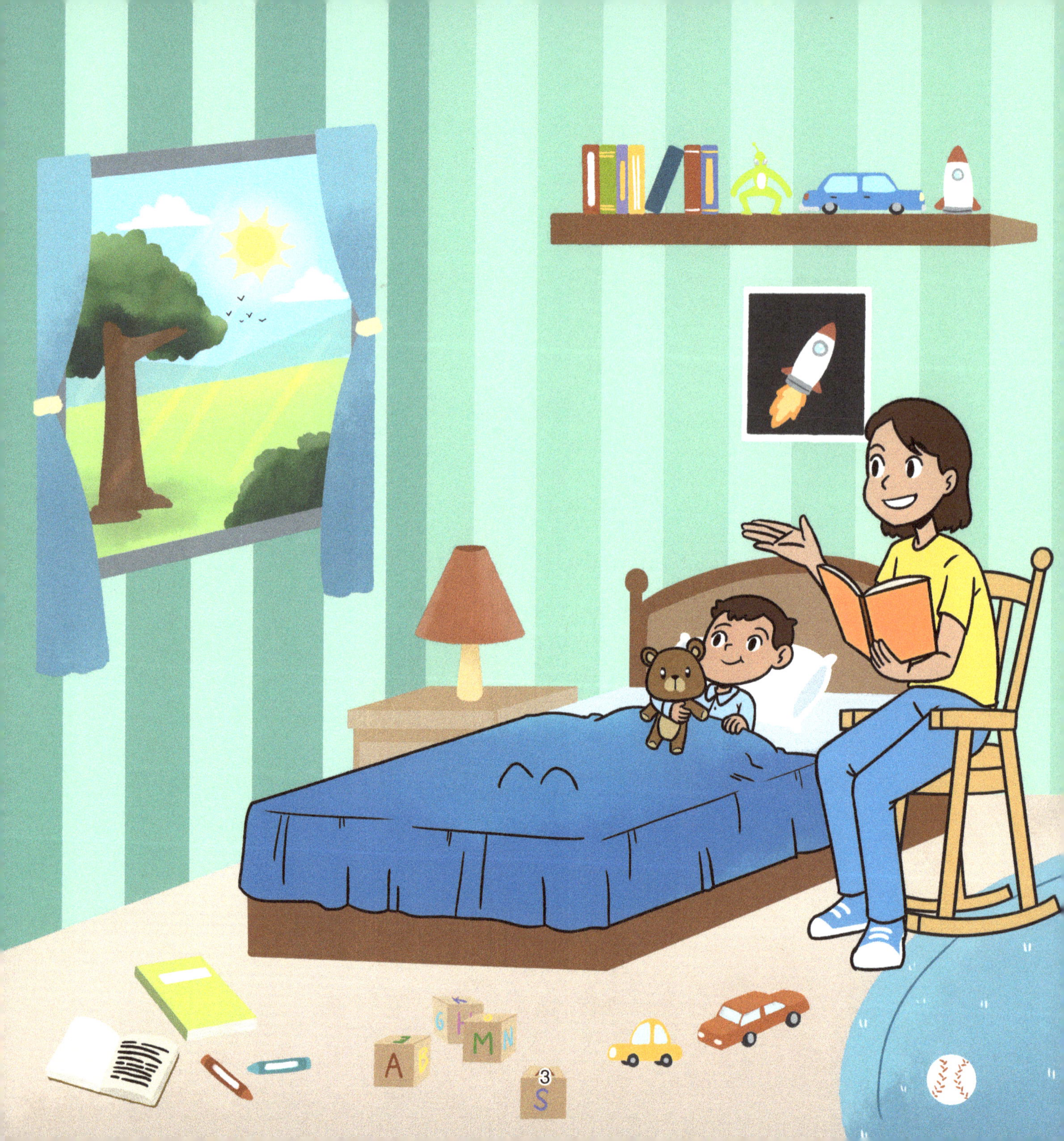

Outside your window is the sun. The sun is shining just for you. The sun is bright to warm you. The sun is watching over you.

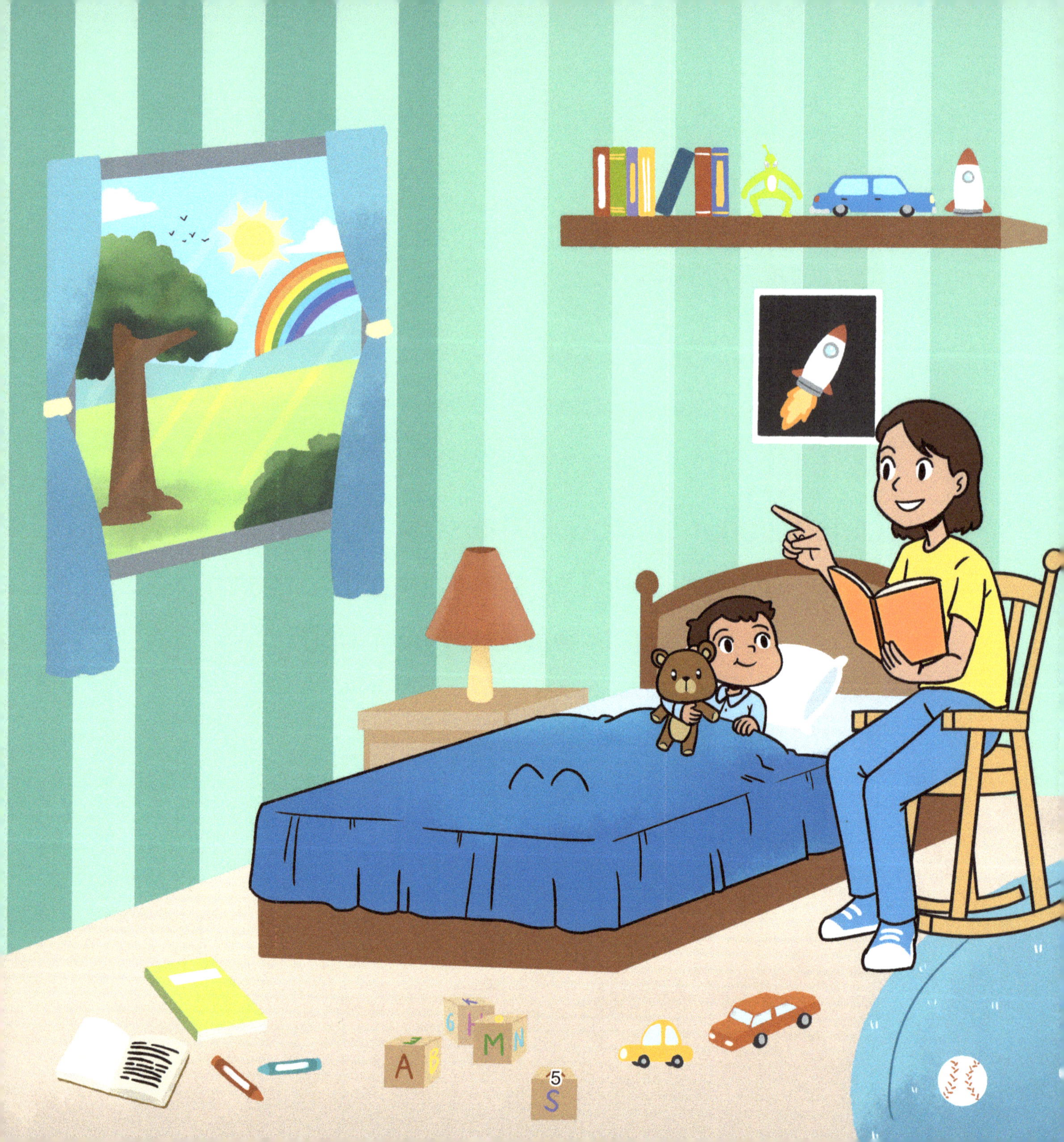

Outside your window is a rainbow. The rainbow is shining just for you. The rainbow is orange, red, and blue. The rainbow is watching over you.

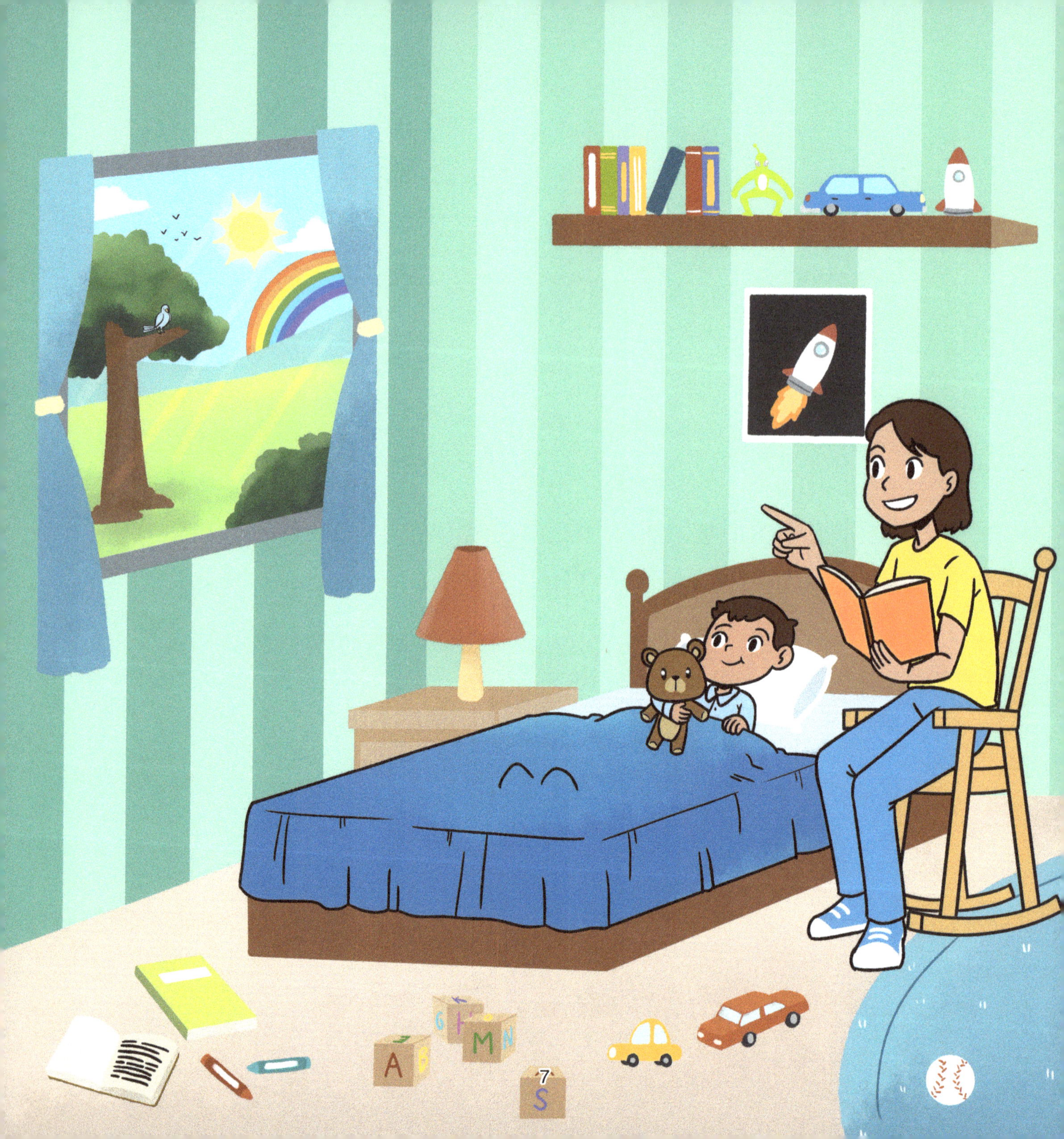

Outside your window is a bird. The bird is singing just for you. The bird is small, just like you. The bird is watching over you.

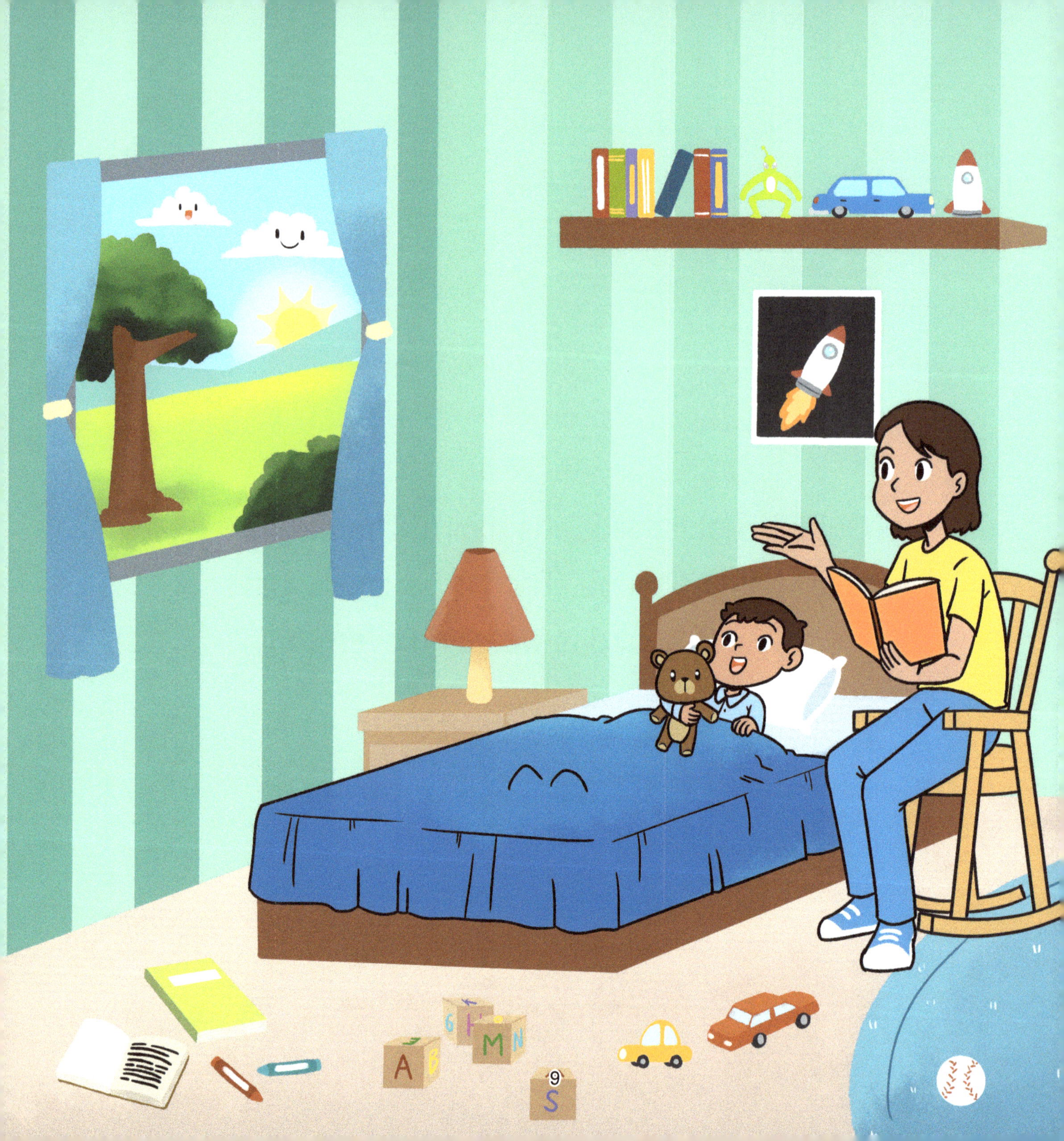

Outside your window is a cloud. The cloud is smiling down at you. The cloud is white, fluffy, and round. The cloud is watching over you.

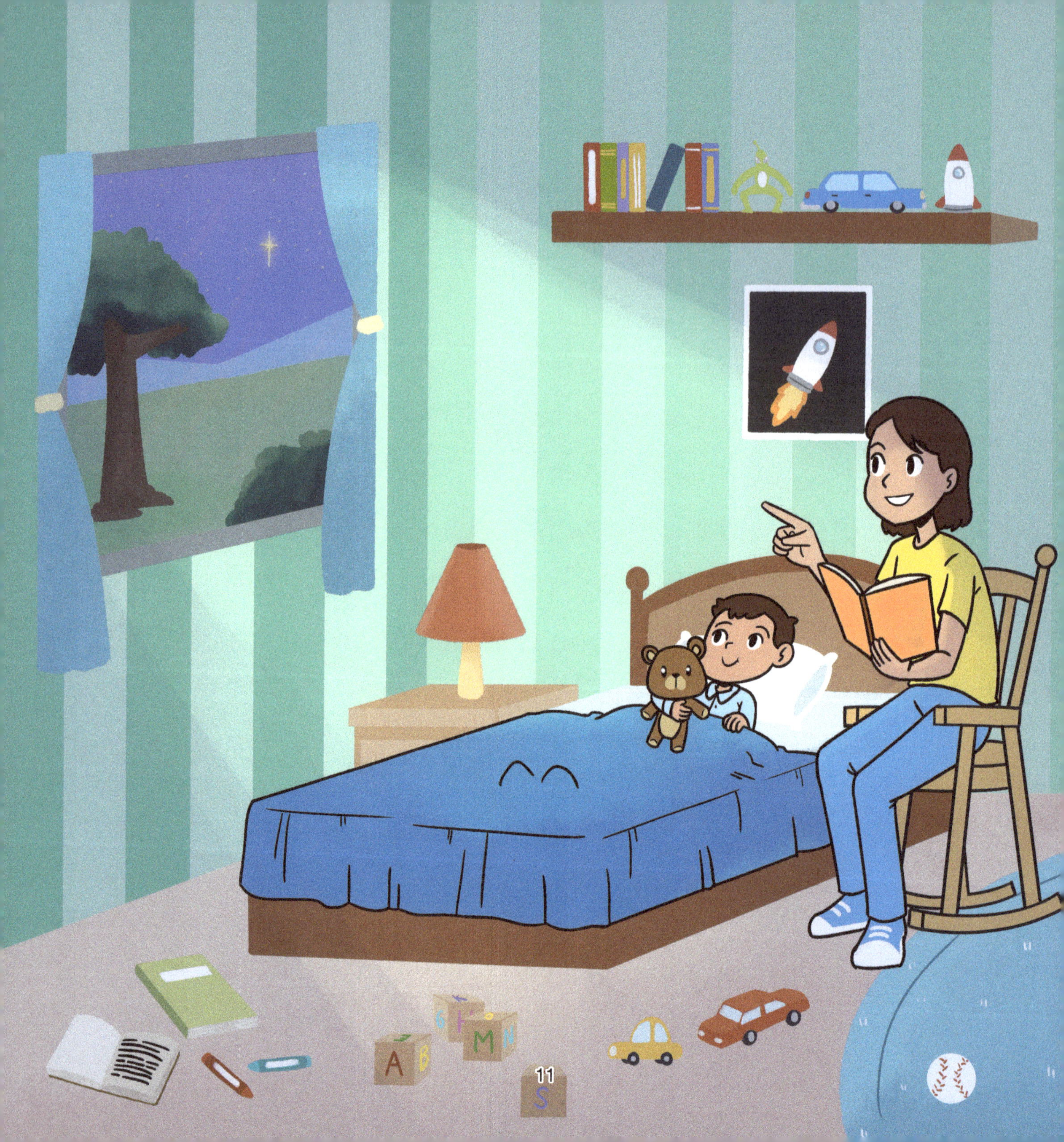

Outside your window is a star. The star is sparkling just for you. The star is bright, twinkling, and blue. The star is watching over you.

13

Outside your window is the moon. The moon is glowing just for you. The moon is round, bright, and new. The moon is watching over you.

15

Outside your window is an angel. The angel is guarding over you. The angel is loyal, safe, and true. The angel is watching over you.

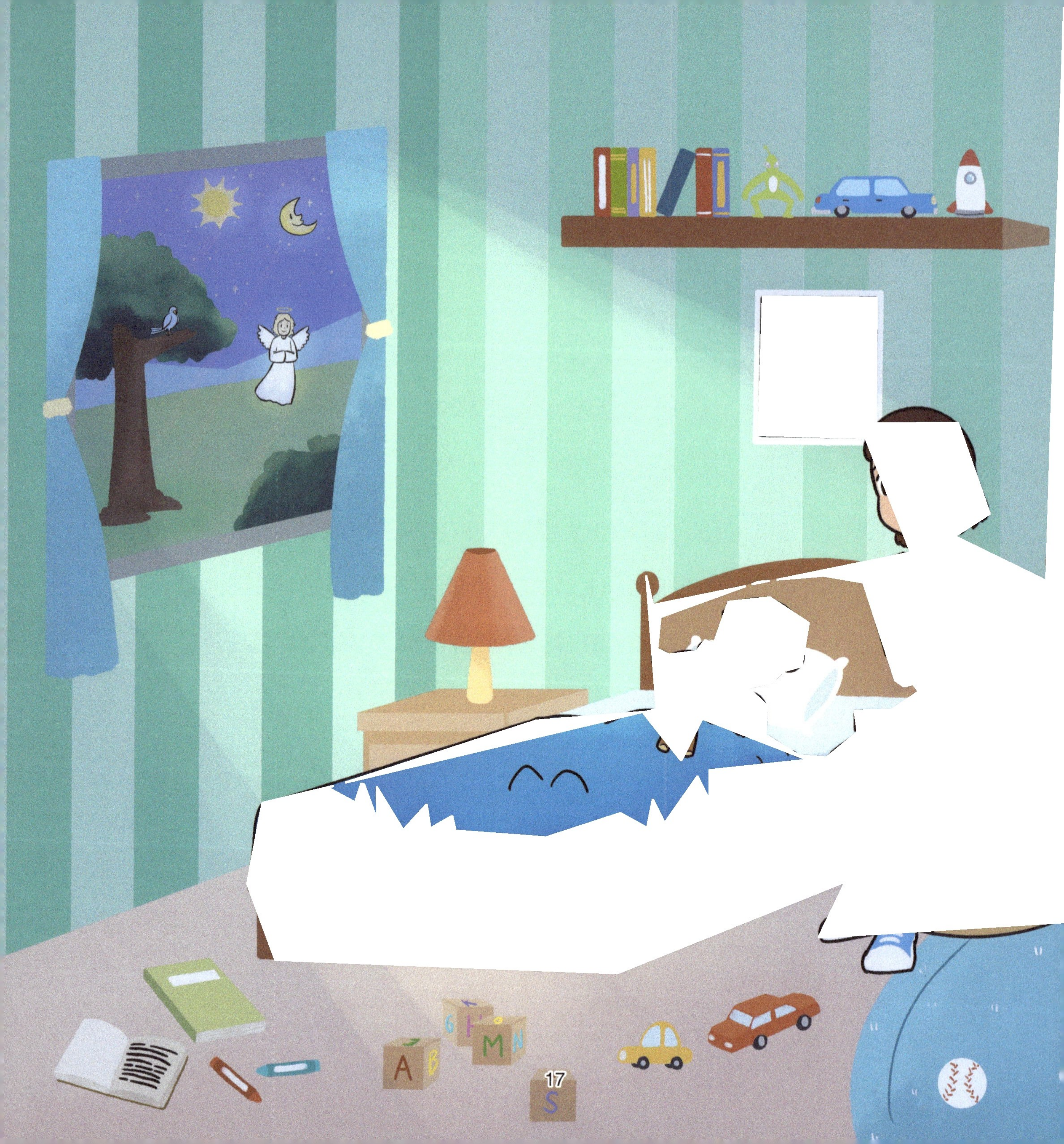

Outside your window is the sun, a bird, the stars, and the moon. Outside your window is an angel; they are all watching over you.

THE END

Angel of God
My Guardian Dear,
To whom His love commits me here,
Ever this day be at my side,
To light and guard, to rule and guide.
Amen

Milton Keynes UK
Ingram Content Group UK Ltd.
UKHW051006121124
451038UK00016B/224